Whispers of Oasis:

Likoo's Poetic Mirage

Whispers of Oasis:
Likoo's Poetic Mirage

Translated by Mahdi Ganjavi & Amin Fatemi

Ethnography by Mansour Alimoradi

ASEMANA
BOOKS

Toronto, Canada

A collaboration between an ethnographer, a bilingual poet, and an Anglo-Irish literature scholar, this multilingual volume includes 100 Likoos, a syllabic genre of oral poetry, in their original Roudbari, accompanied by English and Persian translations.

 The publication of this work has been supported by a 2021 Persian Heritage Foundation grant for publication.

https://asemanabooks.ca/

Contents

Likoo: Syllabic Poetry of Oasis

Mahdi Ganjavi

Likoo is one of the oldest and most concise forms of oral poetry in the Iranian plateau. Composed in the languages of the people of Roudbar and Balochistan in southeast Iran, Likoos are a testament to the cultural diversity and linguistic richness of the region. Balochistan and Roudbar, akin to siblings in geographical proximity, share a profound cultural bond. Despite grappling with challenges such as drought and water scarcity, both regions are adorned with the richness of ancient traditions. The shared cultural heritage extends beyond customary practices, encompassing common legends, epics, and myths. Besides Likoos, which we will discuss in more detail, the cultural convergence of these two regions is evident in indigenous musical expressions, such as "Shayr," (شَیر) compositions that eulogize tribal and community leaders, valorous individuals, and outlaws. These melodic narratives find expression through the voices of chang[1] players, "Pahlavāns," (پهلوان) reflecting a cultural tapestry woven seamlessly across Roudbar and Balochistan. The esteemed artisans known as "Pahlavān" in both Roudbar and Balochistan are recognized as master players. These individuals contribute significantly to the preservation and evolution of the cultural heritage, becoming custodians of the musical traditions that transcend geographical boundaries.

In essence, the shared cultural, historical, and musical tapestry of Balochistan and Roudbar reflects not only the interconnectedness of these regions but also the resilience and continuity of a vibrant heritage that spans generations. The historical nomadic interactions between the denizens of the expansive plains of Roudbar and Jazmurian, and the mountainous and desert landscapes of Balochistan, have fostered a dynamic exchange, resulting in the settlement of numerous Balochi-Roudbari clans in these territories.

8

---

[1] Chang is a traditional stringed instrument with a long, rectangular wooden body and multiple strings stretched across it.

Whispers of Oasis: Likoo's Poetic Mirage

Image: Cameleers of Jazmurian; Photo: Courtesy of Mahdi Mirzaee

As noted, Likoo is one of the forms of oral poetry in both Balochistan and Roudbar. Both Balochi and Roudbari Likoos are syllabic and have rhyming endings, with Roudbari Likoos consisting of five syllables, while Balochi Likoos consists of ten syllables. This poetic form is quite short, but rich in its cultural connotations. Despite the divergence in syllabic structure, both variations of Likoo share a common trait in their brevity. This brevity is not a limitation but rather a strength that demands active participation from the reader. The succinct nature of Likoo poetry requires the audience to become co-creators, actively filling in the spaces between words and syllables with their own interpretations and emotions. This interactive dynamic enhances the cultural significance of Likoo, transforming it from a mere literary form into a shared experience between the poet/reciter and the reader/listener.

Likoos are similar to Haiku, in the sense that both are syllabic, short, filled with images, and are manifestations of daily life as well as ethnic beliefs. However, the two differ in terms of their number and syllabic arrangements, the content of the ethnic beliefs each contains, and the social and natural geography of the people who have composed them. While Haiku is primarily crafted by poets familiar with calligraphy and painting techniques or by Zen Buddhists trained to write this type of poetry, Likoo represents the poetry of ordinary and illiterate people. Likoo predominantly revolves around human and earthly concerns, addressing everyday issues. Furthermore, contrary to Haiku, Likoos do not have seasonal references (kigo) or the specific juxtaposition of words and images in haiku, known as cutting (kiru).

Traditionally, Likoos were sometimes recited by women, and several of them give voice to a woman or are narrated from a female point of view. The recitation of a Likoo is commonly accompanied by musical instruments (such as Qaychak,[2] Chang, Nei Shabani,[3] Donali),[4] and

---

[2] Qaychak or gheychak is a type of bowed lute that is played in Iran, Afghanistan, Pakistan, and Tajikistan.
[3] Shepherd's reed
[4] Donali is a folk instrument hailing from the Balochistan. Donali features two reeds that the musician simultaneously places in their mouth during performance.

at other times, it occurs with no musical instrument but with the mesmerizing and alarming sound of the wind in the desert.

Qaychak. Photo: Courtesy of Mahdi Mirzaee

The content of Likoos mostly consists of romantic longing, grief for death of a youth, separation, and emigration. It explores the anguish of being distant from the motherland and delves into descriptions of the beloved. The word "Likoo" conveys a sense of longing. In some southern regions of Iran, grief and longing are referred to as "Līkah" Līk" and "Lāk."

The birthplace of the Likoos remains shrouded in ambiguity, with no definitive attribution to either Balochistan or Roudbar. The Likoos resonate harmoniously in both regions, encapsulating a shared cultural foundation in both Balochi and Rudbari languages. The name "Likoo," it is argued, originated from the name of a bird. The Likoo bird, a distinctive avian species native to the regions of Roudbar and Balochistan, boasts unique physical attributes that contribute to its fascinating presence in these landscapes. Recognizable by its long, feathered tails and wings adorned with streaks of brown, the Likoo bird possesses a formidable, curved beak. The species is predominantly terrestrial, often observed in small flocks meandering among trees, bushes, or traversing the ground with subtle movements. It has limited flying capabilities, and both males and females share similar physical characteristics.

The Likoo bird is an animated and vocal bird, known for its constant activity and energetic demeanor. It prefers to navigate the ground, employing short and rapid jumps, a characteristic movement that distinguishes it within its habitat. Typically found in the lower reaches of plants, the Likoo bird displays a sociable nature, often congregating in family groups or small flocks, creating a lively presence in the natural setting. When it comes to nesting habits, the Likoo bird exhibits a preference for thorny environments, constructing its nests on bushes, thorn trees, or palm trees. This choice of habitat not only serves as a protective measure but also aligns with its natural inclination towards the varied vegetation present in the regions of Roudbar and Balochistan.

The Likoo bird's significance extends beyond its physical characteristics and behavior, as it is also renowned for its melodic prowess. A singing bird with a voice that resonates across its habitat, the Likoo bird contributes to the auditory tapestry of the landscape.

While the Likoo bird grapples with an uncertain future, precariously perched on the brink of extinction due to the harsh effects of recent droughts (Alimoradi, 2012), its poetic counterpart, Balochi and Roudbari Likoos, have been more fortunate in the last century.

An oasis in the Great Roudbar. Photo: Courtesy of Mahdi Mirzaee

The Balochi Likoo, despite remaining understudied for a considerable period, experienced a transformative turn when Abdulrahman Pahwal translated the Balochi Likoos in 1974. Axenov delved into the study of Likoos among Baloch of Turkmenistan in 1990. Shu'ur categorized Balochi Likoo as one of the eight forms of Afghanistan's oral poetry, drawing parallels between Balochi Likoo and Pashtu Landi (Shu'ur, 2007). In 2005, Momeni published "One Hundred Likoos," the first compilation of a hundred Balochi Likoos along with their Persian translation, shedding light on the structure and content of Balochi Likoo. Balochi Likoo is also an oral poetry passed down among the Baloch people. Its words closely resemble everyday language. Persian words have found their way into the Balochi Likoos due to the influence of both languages on each other. Love is also one of the main themes of Balochi Likoos, primarily focusing on real and everyday love rather than spiritual/religious one. Although women's voices are not often expressed in this form of poetry, women are the subject of longing in many of the Likoos. Movement is also a significant aspect of Balochi Likoos. Various means of movement and travel, including modern inventions like airplanes and motorcycles, appear frequently within it. In sum, Balochi Likoo represents the history and social conditions of the Baloch people (Momeni, 2009; also see Afrashi, 2008).

Roudbari Likoo, however, remained understudied until Alimoradi's efforts to record and study this tradition. As this volume is introducing Roudbari Likoos to the English-speaking world for the first time, some words on the Roudbar would be necessary. With a population of about 700,000, Roudbar has unique cultural-geographical characteristics. It is at the confluence of the littoral culture of Hormozgan in the Persian Gulf, the Persian culture of Kerman, and the Balochi culture of Balochistan. Immigration within the plateau, combined with the relative inaccessibility, has made Roudbar ethno-culturally and linguistically distinctive.

The Great Roudbar includes the cities of Roudbar-e Junubi, Qaleh Ganj, Manujan, Kahnuj, Faryab, and the plains of Jiroft and Anbarabad in the south of Kerman. Most of these cities were established on the banks of Halil River, around which a very ancient civilization flourished. Due to the supreme meadows and pastures, fertile soil, and abundant water along the Halil River— the largest river in the southeast of Iran—, numerous tribes from all over Iranian plateau migrated to these areas over time. They brought with them their culture, manners, and arts, enriching the banks of the Halil River with a diverse tapestry of traditions.

People in the Great Roudbar speak several main languages: "Aram-Nāram" (أَرَم-نارَم), "Kurtah" (گُرتَه) "Balochi," Birāhū'ī (براهویی) and "Persian." "Aram-Naram", which is also known as "Roudbari" is a language related to both the dialect of the Hormozgan people and the Balochi language, serving as the dominant language in the Great Roudbar region. Geographically, "Aram-Nāram" or "Roudbari" is considered the link between Persian and Balochi languages. Its application is limited from the south, where the Balochi language is predominant, to the north, where Persian is commonly used. Roudbari's limited contact with the country's lingua franca, Persian, has helped preserve its distinctive characteristics (Motallebi, 2015). From a genealogical perspective, Roudbari and its geographical varieties are placed in the group of Bashkardi dialects, which is "a collective designation for numerous dialects spoken in southeastern Iran." (Skjærvø, 1988)

Roudbari Likoos are commonly made up of four words, with ending rhyme. Because of its unique characteristics, Roudbari Likoo is used in a variety of poetic expressions, including mourning songs, hymns, as well as songs of happiness and epic narratives. Likoo is a folk poem, and several of the natives in the area have written at least one or two Likoos during their life. Usually, no money is received for singing and playing Likoos. However, as noted earlier a small group of veteran Qaychak players, known locally as "Pahlavāns", and some Sorna[5] players who play wedding music, receive a fee. For example, "Pahlavāns" incorporate Likoo into their performances between the recitation of certain epic verses to prevent the narration from becoming tedious and monotonous. But mostly, Likoos are written and recited by ordinary people without any pay. Based on the style in which Likoos are recited and performed, they are known by different names in the Roudbar region, such as Dahū (دهو), Dahū Zahrā (دهو زهرا), Dīkan (دیکن), Zaḥīrūkī (زحیروکی), and Taskīn (تسکین).

Likoos echo the lives of people in Roudbar, the lives of those living in the oasis, surrounded by the desert. They depict life in the desert with all its hardships, challenges, and failures. Likoos are the poetry of short joys and continuous hardship, reflecting the brutality of life

---

[5] Sorna is a woodwind instrument played in various places in Iran including Luristan, Kurdistan, and Sistan.

dominated by nomadic social relations. They are the voice of a lover who catches a glimpse of his beloved in the desert, the call of a camel driver in the lonely nights of the desert on a dry path, or the mourning over the death of a young person due to tribal violence.

Kalpooregoo hot springs. Photo: Courtesy of Mahdi Mirzaee

Likoo and the Poetry of Indigenous and Minoritized Iranians

Likoos, as one of the oldest and most concise forms of oral poetry in the Iranian plateau, serve as a gateway to a broader tapestry of indigenous poetic traditions in Iran. Persian classical poetry enjoys a revered status on the global literary stage. Renowned for its rich history, intricate rhyme schemes, and profound philosophical and mystical depth, Persian poetry has garnered widespread recognition among scholars and enthusiasts worldwide. The works of iconic Persian poets such as Rumi, Hafez, and Saadi have been translated into numerous languages, allowing a global audience to appreciate the beauty and wisdom embedded in their verses. Moreover, academic institutions around the world have dedicated comprehensive studies to Persian poetry, exploring its cultural, historical, and linguistic dimensions.

In contrast to the well-explored realm of Persian poetry, many indigenous and minoritized[6] poetic forms of the Iranian plateau remain relatively uncharted on the global stage. These lesser-known traditions, steeped in cultural nuances and unique expressions, await scholarly exploration and global readership to foster a more inclusive and diverse literary landscape.

Beyond the enchanting verses of Likoos, indigenous poetry in Iran manifests itself in a multitude of expressions, each carrying the unique imprint of its cultural context. For instance, the Amiri tradition, native to Iran's Mazandaran region, weaves together linguistic nuances and regional flavors, offering a poetic lens into the cultural intricacies of Mazandaran. Similarly, the Chahardaneh, Sarhadi, and Haqiqi forms each unfold as vibrant threads in the

---

[6] Minority literature, as the name suggests, revolves around the literary expressions of a group of marginalized people in contrast to certain dominant forms. It has been used to identify literary works of groups who have been marginalized based on their race, language, ethnicity, gender identity and orientation, socio-economic status, and geographical location, just to mention a few instances. A common element is a degree of marginalization and imposition from the wider and more established majority.

tapestry of indigenous poetry, representing diverse perspectives and historical narratives.

Other indigenous traditions such as Gūranī (گورانی), a form of Kurdish poetry comprising one or two verses, and Bayt (بیت), a specifically Kurdish poetry in Kurmanji Kurdish, underscore the linguistic diversity inherent in Iran's indigenous poetic traditions. These forms resonate with the distinctive rhythms and cultural nuances of the Kurdish communities, enriching the overall mosaic of Iranian indigenous poetry. Furthermore, Chahārlingī (چهارلنگی), comprising verses in the Luri dialect, contributes to this diverse collection, showcasing the linguistic and cultural wealth embedded in the oral traditions of the Lur people.[7]

19

Despite their profound historical roots and cultural significance, these forms of indigenous poetry have been subject to limited scholarly attention. The 19th century saw European orientalists, including Valentin Zhukovski, embark on the initial exploration of these poetic traditions. Subsequently, in the early twentieth century and in the aftermath of the Constitutional Revolution in Iran (1906), local scholars such as Kuhi Kermani, Ebrahim Shakurzadeh, Mohammad Mukri, and Sadeq Hedayat began compiling and studying these

---

[7] Other notable forms of indigenous poetry in Iran, include Siā wa Chāmānah (سیا و چمانه), a syllabic poetry in Hawrami Kurdish, Chārdānah,(چاردانه) in Gilaki language, and Bāyātī (بایاتی), a syllabic poetry in Azerbaijani Turkish.

poems, marking a pivotal moment in the scholarly engagement with indigenous poetry (Zulfaghari and Ahmadi, 2009).[8]

The exploration of Iran's indigenous poetry serves not only to diversify cultural expressions but also to complicate our understanding of poetic forms, traditions, aesthetics, and the very essence of poetry itself. Iran's indigenous poetry, such as Likoos introduced here, often crafted by anonymous poets, and perpetually refined through oral traditions, plays a pivotal role in fostering a communal understanding of the significance of poetry within a culture. The communal nature of indigenous poetry, manifested in its collective creation and continuous evolution, encourages a deeper engagement with the multifaceted roles that poetry plays in communities. Rather than individualistic endeavors, these poems emerge from the collective consciousness of a community.

The lack of a singular author allows the poems to belong to the community at large, emphasizing the communal ownership of cultural narratives and expressions. Passed down through generations, poems become living entities that evolve over time. Each

---

[8] One contentious point among researchers revolves around the metric scale of these indigenous songs, with disagreements on whether it is syllabic or metric. Scholars such as Adib Tusi assert the metric nature, while others, such as Bahar, argue for syllabic structures gradually converging with Arabic metric prosody. Khanlari introduces a unique perspective by emphasizing the importance of both their syllabic and phonetical characteristic and the role of accent in their prosody. Vahidian Kamiyar, in his work on the meter of folk poetry, contends that stress does not significantly influence Persian poetry's prosody, advocating that these poetic traditions follow a more liberal usage of metric poetry. Tabibzadeh challenges the notion that prosody is based on the quantity of vowels, asserting that composers of folk poetry learn it informally, with formal learning being necessary for producing metric works (Tabibzadeh, 2003:45).

recitation becomes an opportunity for the community to actively participate in the preservation and reshaping of cultural narratives. This ongoing process of refinement ensures that the poetry remains relevant and resonant within the community, fostering a sense of continuity and shared heritage. Furthermore, the communal understanding of poetry within indigenous cultures challenges conventional Western and capitalist modern notions that often prioritize individual authorship and recognition. In these communities, the emphasis is on the collective, with poetry functioning as a communal thread that not only serves as a source of aesthetic enjoyment but also as a repository of cultural memory, social commentary, and spiritual reflection.

21

Besides understanding Likoos as indigenous poetry, categorizing them under minoritized poetry aids in further comprehending their marginalization. Similar to many other forms of minority literature, Likoo possesses a unique stance by sharing some general aspects characteristic of such literature while maintaining its distinctive and specific characteristics. A defining aspect of minoritized languages and their literature has been the threat to their very existence.[9] Alongside explicitly banning an entire language, another favorite tool is to 'downgrade' a language to a dialect in an attempt to make it a

---

[9] Examples include the ban on the use of the Irish language by the British throughout centuries (Doyle, 2015), Franco's ban on Basque, Catalan, and Galician, which was so extreme that priests were sometimes chastised for pronouncing Latin with a non-Castilian accent (Claesson, 2022).

part of the realm of the official language. Such is the case with Roudbari Likoos.

Writing in a minoritized language surrounded by an official language environment poses its own unique set of challenges. Cergol describes one of these challenges in following terms:

> In a minority literature, language acquires a particular valency, which even matures into a value. The value of language is otherwise closely related to the value of ethnicity since it is the bearer of the existential dimension. There is a feeling expressed in works written by minority members which they all share in common: it is the feeling that they will never be able to be perfectly fluent in their mother tongue, which they are forced to learn with difficulty in an environment that does not use that language (Cergol, 2016, p. 71).

It is no wonder that minority literature was not historically included in official canons. The very need for a canon, at least historically, defies its relationship with the language of a minority in its sovereignty. An example from the origins of the English Canon might be helpful; scholars disagree on an exact date for the birth of the English Canon but mostly agree that the idea was put to use "in the constitutional bolstering of the late eighteenth and early nineteenth century when a coherent set of cultural values was urgently demanded (Gardiner, 2013, p. 3)."[10] When canons of world literature first started

---

[10] Even if the ever-present socio-political issues, matters of literacy, lack of opportunities for expression, and an unrecorded oral tradition had not been reason enough for marginalization and misrepresentation, this new set of cultural values, worthy only of the posh, white English gentleman, linguistically and culturally,

to appear, they were mostly, if not exclusively, comprised of works of literature written in the official or prominent language of an underrepresented country.[11]

The exploration of poetry of minoritized Iranians contributes significantly to the formation of a literary understanding that is inherently multilingual and characterized by diverse modes of poetic expression and experience.

Unsettling and Expanding the Canons

The marginalization of indigenous poetry in Iran is rooted in part in the ascendancy and dominance of Persian metric poetry during the Islamic era (Sutton, 1975; de Bruijn, 2008). Delving into the annals of Iranian literary history, the prominence of Persian metric poetry emerges as a pivotal factor that shaped the literary landscape and, inadvertently, relegated indigenous poetic traditions to the periphery. After the Arab conquest and gradual conversion of the majority of people in this plateau to Islam, the syllabic poetic tradition was replaced by the Arabic metric tradition as poetry came under the influence of Islamic culture (de Fouchécour, 2006). The Islamic era

23

---

prevented the inclusion of any non-English literary work from any other part of the British Empire at home or abroad.

[11] Take, for instance, the first edition of The Norton Anthology of World Literature

witnessed the flourishing of Persian poetry, largely influenced by classical Arabic poetic forms and structures.[12]

As Persian metric poetry gained ascendancy, it became not only a literary medium but also a marker of cultural prestige and sophistication. This elevation in status led to the gradual eclipsing of indigenous poetic traditions, which found their roots in regional languages and dialects. The standardization and institutionalization of Persian metric poetry further marginalized alternative poetic forms, creating a hierarchy within the literary canon.

This historical analysis unveils the intricate interplay between language, power, and cultural hegemony. The dominance of Persian metric poetry, while contributing significantly to the richness of Iranian literary heritage, inadvertently marginalized diverse indigenous poetic traditions. Recognizing and addressing this historical trajectory is essential for working towards a more inclusive appreciation of the multitude of poetic expressions that form the mosaic of Iran's rich literary tapestry.

Zulfaghari and Ahmadi (2009) posit that pre-Islamic Iran lacked metric poetry, asserting that the indigenous forms, with their syllabic prosody, are a continuation of the melodious local songs that distinguished themselves from prose in the pre-Islamic period. These

---

[12] The rise of Persian metric poetry is attributed to the political and linguistic assertion of independence by semi-autonomous non-Arab governments vis-à-vis Arab authority. Persian metric poetry became a potent tool for government propaganda, and metric poetry played a pivotal role in standardizing the Persian language (Tabibzadeh, 2010).

indigenous forms continued to be produced, and mainly orally transmitted within various communities. Despite the resilience of these indigenous poetic traditions, the advent of the modern era, particularly the nation-state building process, ushered in a complex phase in their trajectory. Instead of being integrated into the creation of a national literature, these traditions faced marginalization and a process of indigenization. The exclusion from the construction of the national literary identity resulted in the further sidelining of these indigenous forms, stifling their potential for broader recognition and appreciation.

The dominance of official language often reflects power dynamics and reinforces the cultural hegemony of a particular group, leading to the neglect of alternative linguistic expressions. The process of nation-state building includes attempts at constructing national literatures. This process has also been studied in the case of the formation of history of literature as a genre (Jabbari, 2023). Also, the transition from multilingualism to the imposition of a formal language within the context of nation-state building carries significant implications for the recognition and status of poetry in languages other than the designated official language. As modern Iranian governments strived to create a unified national identity, they often prioritized the establishment of a singular Persian linguistic framework, sidelining the rich diversity of regional and minority languages. Consequently, numerous poetic traditions composed in these marginalized languages find themselves excluded from achieving national status. As a result, the poetic traditions rooted in these languages face systemic barriers in gaining recognition, appreciation, and preservation even in the national realm, as evident in the case of Likoos, which is the subject of this book. The political and social conditions underpinning this linguistic homogenization further marginalize these unique forms of poetry, limiting their accessibility and perpetuating a narrative that prioritizes Persian cultural and linguistic perspectives over others.

About This Translation

The Likoos presented in this translation are based on the dedicated ethnographical efforts of Mansour Alimoradi. Alimoradi's endeavor represents a passionate and personal commitment to preserving and showcasing the rich oral tradition of the Roudbari community. His role as a cultural custodian becomes particularly significant as he embarks on a profound ethnological journey, traversing the cultural landscapes of the region.

Alimoradi's involvement in collecting and introducing Likoos started back in 1998 and continues to this date. His involvement extends beyond the confines of academic curiosity; it is rooted in a genuine connection with the people and the poetic traditions of Roudbar. His engagement with this oral tradition is marked by a hands-on approach, involving personal journeys through the diverse terrains of the region. These journeys, undertaken with a keen ethnographic eye, allow Alimoradi to immerse himself in the lived experiences of the

Roudbari community, forging a direct connection with the poets, storytellers, and guardians of this vibrant cultural heritage.

Sandy regions of Turig, near Qaleh Ganj. Photo: Courtesy of Mahdi Mirzaee

27

Furthermore, Alimoradi's commitment extends to meticulous work with records available in the region. His scholarly pursuits involve not only the recording and translation of the oral tradition into Persian but also a careful examination of historical manuscripts, documents, and any available records that shed light on the evolution and preservation of Likoos. Collecting several hundred authentic Likoos required constant travel, research, and inquiries. Some of the Likoos in this volume were recorded and transcribed by Alimoradi nearly two decades ago, at a time when there were not as many communication facilities, and the virtual communication tools had not yet flourished to ease certain research and networking difficulties.

As a bilingual Roudbari and Persian language poet, Alimoradi serves as a bridge between the Roudbar's oral tradition and a broader Persian-speaking audience. His translations of Likoos into Persian not only made these poetic gems accessible to a wider readership but also contributed to a broader understanding of the cultural diversity within Iran.

What began as the publication of Likoos and their Persian translations[13] has evolved into a cultural phenomenon with a reach far beyond the confines of a book. There's a significant resurgence of the Roudbari likoo, gaining momentum as local poets contribute to its revival, spurred by the newfound visibility it has earned. Simultaneously, this transformative journey has triggered a surge of inspiration among Persian poets who, captivated by Likoos, now infuse their work with the essence of this tradition.

The Likoo, once tethered to the specific cultural context of Roudbar, has broken free from geographical constraints, imprinting its influence on Persian modern poetry in unexpected and profound ways. The reverberations of Likoos resonate through the creative landscape, fostering a dynamic interplay between indigenous

---

[13] Alimoradi's collection and Persian translation of Roudbari Likoos are published in two separate volumes in Iran; see Alimoradi, Likoo's of Roudbar-e Jonoub, Tehran: Nun. Vol 1, 2012; Vol 2, 2015.

traditions and modern and contemporary Persian expression. This phenomenon not only underscores the enduring power of Likoos but also serves as a testament to the profound impact that cultural revitalization can have on artistic innovation.

The meanings embedded in indigenous poetry are intricately woven into the fabric of local histories, traditions, and worldviews, presenting a challenge to translators and scholars attempting to convey the depth of these verses to a global audience.

Most of the Likoos in the present collection are translated from Aram Naram, a language also known as Roudbari. Among the collected Likoos, a hundred were selected that you will read in this collection. Some Likoos were left out because they referred to the subject, place, event, and specific regional characters, and their atmosphere was not very tangible even for the non-southern readers inside Iran. The poems in this book have been collected from the residents of Marz rural district, Rameshk city, Qaleh Ganj, Jiroft, Anbarabad, Faryab, Kahnuj, Manujan counties in southern Kerman, and Iranshahr and Delgan counties in western Baluchistan.

30   Map of the regions from which the Likos in this book have been collected.

Alimoradi have heard most of them either from local musicians and singers of Likoo, or have transcribed them from old cassette tapes, some of which were recorded forty to fifty years ago by tape recorders of the time.

Mansour Alimoradi (in white) in the company of Fereydon Jafari, chang player, and
Rahman Jafari (left), a Likoo reciter from Chah Hieshvarki village in Qaleh Ganj.
Photo: Courtesy of Mahdi Mirzaee

The English translations are done by Amin Fatemi and I. Amin
Fatemi is a multifaceted individual, wielding skills as a translator,
educator, and Irish literature scholar based in Reading. His extensive
endeavors have primarily focused on delving into the rich tapestry of
Irish indigenous poetry. In tandem, I have contributed to the Persian
literary landscape by translating into Persian a broad range of works,
including high modernist, eco-poetry, and New York School English
poetry.

Adding a personal dimension to our collaborative efforts, both Amin
and I are born in Kerman province and share a deep appreciation for
the land and its people. This shared background infuses our

translations with a nuanced understanding of the cultural context, enriching the poetic expressions we work to convey.

To further immerse myself in the essence of Likoos, I had the privilege of being hosted by Alimoradi on a journey to Roudbar. This enriching experience provided invaluable opportunities to meet Likoo reciters in person, engaging in insightful discussions about Likoo culture and poetry. These encounters not only deepened my understanding but also infused our translations with a more profound appreciation for the living breathing tradition that is Likoo poetry.

It is crucial to acknowledge that the translations within this volume, while aspiring to offer a solid understanding of Likoos, should not be viewed through a strictly scholarly lens. Rather, our combined endeavors have been geared towards conveying and introducing the rich poetic tradition of Likoos to the general reader. Our primary aim is to bridge the gap between this culturally significant tradition and a wider audience, fostering appreciation and understanding among those who may not be steeped in the academic nuances of scholarly work. In doing so, we hope to share the beauty, depth, and cultural significance of Likoos with a broader readership, transcending the boundaries of specialized scholarship.

Drawing on Alimoradi's expertise, we leaned on his poetic translations from Roudbari to Persian as a solid foundation. Simultaneously, we maintained a close connection to the original Roudbari, paying particular attention to its musicality and the unique terms embedded within it. These linguistic intricacies sometimes echo the distinctive Kermani dialect of Persian, lending an authentic touch to our translations.

During the translation process, our goal has been to stay attentive to the original text while bringing the cultural and social connotations of the poems into English. Our paramount objective has been to maintain a delicate balance, ensuring both fidelity to the original text and the nuanced conveyance of the cultural and social connotations embedded within these poems into English. This commitment arises from a recognition of the intrinsic connection between language and culture, acknowledging that poetry, as a vessel of cultural expression, carries a wealth of meaning beyond the literal interpretation of words. To achieve this, we engage in a close exploration of the linguistic and thematic intricacies of the original verses, considering the historical context, socio-political nuances, and the distinctive aesthetics that characterize each form of indigenous poetry. This contextual understanding becomes the guiding thread in our translation efforts, allowing us to render not just the literal meanings of the verses but also the emotional and cultural resonances that imbue them. In essence, our translation process is a dynamic interplay between linguistic precision and cultural sensitivity. We recognize that these indigenous poems are not merely linguistic artifacts but living expressions of the diverse cultures they represent.

In our earnest endeavor to cultivate a culture of multilinguality and inclusivity, this volume is crafted as a multilingual work. Within its

33

pages, readers will encounter Alimoradi's Persian translations alongside the original Roudbari text and Amin's and my English translations. This intentional inclusion of multiple languages serves as a lens through which indigenous poetry can inhabit a more expansive and resonant space. We firmly believe that multilinguality is not merely a practical consideration but an essential element in capturing the essence of indigenous poetic traditions. By presenting Likoos in Roudbari, Persian, and English, we aspire to provide an immersive experience that resonates with a diverse readership. This approach is a celebration of linguistic diversity and a recognition of the interconnectedness of cultures.

Out of the 100 Likoos featured in this collection, 39 have previously appeared in Asymptote, while 4 have found a place in Modern Poetry in Translation. Notably, 12 of these poems were also reprinted in Essential Voices, Poetry of Iran and Its Diaspora, edited by Christopher Nelson and published by Green Linden Press in 2021. The rest are appearing for the first time in English.

We suggest that readers also take the time to listen to recitations of Likoos, available on Asemana Books' YouTube Channel. This link directs you to a short Likoo music file from an audio tape that Alimoradi managed to make a copy of in 1998 and later digitize.[14] The singer's name is Alijan, and he resided in the Chah Kichi area, a rural region situated between Roudbar-e Jonoub and Balochistan.

---

[14] https://www.youtube.com/watch?v=zi3CSRUZuMY

Alijan was one of the prominent reciters of Likoos in the Roudbar and Balochistan regions.

The second link is related to a musical recitation of Likoo by Shir Mohammad Espandar, a renowned Baloch musician who resides in Bampur city, in Iran's Balochistan.[15] The third link also takes you to Alimoradi's recitation of several Likoos in original Roudbari.[16] We hope that listening to these files will help readers further immerse themselves in the world of Likoos.

The publication of this work has been made possible through the generous support of a grant from the Persian Heritage Foundation, an organization dedicated to the preservation and promotion of Persian cultural heritage. In expressing profound gratitude, I extend sincere thanks to Mohammad Mehdi Khorrami and Houra Yavari for their unwavering intellectual support for this project. Special acknowledgment is owed to Ali Gheissari for his kindness and mentorship, which have significantly contributed to the realization of this endeavor. We are also grateful to Mahmood Khoshchehreh, Blair Kuntz, Viola Alberti, Antonio Gambacorta, Andrea Romanzi, Peter Robinson, James Wagstaffe, and Nuzhat Abbas for reading the drafts of the translations and providing valuable comments. Mahdi Mirzaee kindly shared several mesmerizing photos of Roudbar with us. A heartfelt expression of gratitude is extended to the Persian Heritage

---

[15] https://www.youtube.com/watch?v=YEXNcsrwtc0
[16] https://www.youtube.com/watch?v=Xa5E87XKxnU

Foundation Awards Committee for placing their trust in this project. Their recognition of the cultural significance of Roudbari Likoos and their support in the form of this grant underscore the collective commitment to preserving and disseminating the diverse cultural heritage embedded in Iran's oral traditions. We hope that this study and translation help advance the understanding and appreciation of Iran's cultural diversity, as well as providing insight into the verse of the people of the oasis and their challenging lives and exquisite imagination in the desert.

References:

Azarang, A.H. (2016). Khanlari Parviz, *Encyclopædia Iranica*, online edition.

Adib Tusi, M. A. (1953). Tarāna-hā-yi maḥalī. *Majalah dānishkadeh 'adabīyāt tabriz*, 5(1), 40-52.

Afrashi, A. (2008). 'ishārātī bar taḥlīl sākhtārī-muhtavāeī līku, shi'r shafāhī baluchī. *Nashrīyah zabān wa zabānshināsī*, 7, 27-39

Ahmad Panahi, M. (2004). *Tarānah wa tarānah surā 'ī dar īrān*. Tehran: Surush.

Alimoradi, M. (2015). *'ash'ār wa tarānihāy-i mardumān ḥawzah halīl rūd*. Kerman: Farhang Ameh.

Alimoradi, M. (2014). *likūhā, kūtāhtarīn surūdihāy-i shafāhī īrān (Vol 2)*. Tehran: Nun.

Alimoradi, M. (2012). *likūhā, kūtāhtarīn surūdihāy-i shafāhī īrān (Vol 1)*. Tehran: Nun.

Axenov, S. (1990). Liko in the poetical folk art of the Baluch of Turkmenistan. In A.V. Rossi (Ed.), *Newsletter of Baluchistan Studies* (pp. 3-14). Rome, Instituto Italiano per il Medio ed Estremo Oriente (ISMEO).

Bahar, M. T. (1972). *Bahār wa adab fārsī*. Tehran: Jibi.

de Bruijn, J. T. P. (Ed.). (2008). *General introduction to Persian literature* (First edition.). I.B. Tauris.

Cergol, J. (2016). Some typological features of 'minority' literature: the case of the Slovenian and Italian minorities. *L'Analisi Linguistica e Letteraria*, 61–76.

Claesson, C. (2022). Vernacular resistance: Catalan, Basque, and Galician opposition to Francoist monolingualism. In C. Kullberg, & D. Watson (Eds.), *Vernaculars in an Age of World Literatures* (pp. 51-80). (Bloomsbury Academic). Bloomsbury Publishing.

Doyle, A. (2015). *A history of the Irish language: From the Norman invasion to independence*. Oxford University Press.

de Fouchécour C.H. (2006). Persian literature classical, *Encyclopædia Iranica*, XIII, Fasc. 4, pp. 414-432.

Ganjavi, M. & Fatemi, A. (Trans.) (2020). Lickos: Syllabic poetry of the oasis. *Asymptote*.

Ganjavi, M. & Fatemi, A. (Trans.) (2020). Four Lickos. *Modern Poetry in Translation*.

Gardiner, M. (2013*). The constitution of English literature.* In *Bloomsbury Publishing (UK) eBooks*.

Jabbari, A. (2023). *The making of Persianate modernity: Language and literary history between Iran and India* (1st ed., Vol. 25). Cambridge University Press.

Natel Khanlari, P. (1966). *wazn shiʿr fārsī*. Tehran: Bunyad Farhang Iran.

Momeni, M. (2009). *ṣad likū, surūdihāyi balūchī*. Tehran: Meshki.

Motallebi, M. (2015). A linguistic study of Rudbari dialect of Kerman. *Journal of the Faculty of Letters and Humanities*, 17(36), 269-305.

Skjærvø, P. O. (1988). BAŠKARDI, *Encyclopedia Iranica.*

Sutton, L. P. E. (1975). The foundations of Persian prosody and metrics. *Iran: Journal of the British Institute of Persian Studies, 13*, 75–97.

Tabibzadeh, O. (2010). *Barrisī taṭbīqī wazn-hāyi kamī wa tekīya'ī-hijā'ī dar fārsī wa gīlakī. Adab pazhuhī*,11, 8-30.

Zulfaghari, H. & Ahmadi, L. (2009). Gūnahshināsī būmī surūdhāy-i īrān, *Adab pazhuhī*, 7-8, 143-170.

100 Likoos

دلِ ظُهرِ گرما
نَتگُ بفرما

در آن ظهر داغ تابستان
تعارفم نکردی که بنشینم

In that hot summer noon
You did not invite me to sit down

دِهن دَر کلیدِن
دور و برُم لوتن

قفلی بر در
دور و برم
خلوت و خاموش

A lock on the door!
All around me
Calm and quiet

كَوتُم رو رَندِت
كَوتَر دستبندِت

44

روی ردت افتادم
دست‌بندت افتاده بود

I followed your tracks
Your bracelet was dropped on the ground

پرچَم سر کبُن
تاکی بِصبرُم؟

پرچمی بر سر گورستان
تا به کی باید تحمل کرد؟

Another flag placed in the graveyard
How long can I suffer?

سر چاهِ گِرآوِن
چادِن گَر خُواوِن

سر چاه تلخ آب
دختری با چادر خاکستری
در خواب

Beside the bitter water well
A girl in a gray chador
Is asleep

نِشتُم لَوجوی خُشک
سر وادَهی سَحبُشک

لب جوی خشکی نشسته‌ام   **47**
سر وعده‌ی سیاه‌گیسو

I sit beside a desert river
Waiting for the dark-haired beloved
Who promised

چادِنت اَ جُنُم
بی تو نامُنُم

چادرت را بر سر کشیده‌ام
بدون تو می‌میرم

I've pulled your chador over my head
Without you I can't survive

ئی حور وَر آ حور
دوستی نابو زور

از این دره تا درەی دیگر
دوستی به زور نمی‌شود

You can't force friendship
From one valley to the other

جَمکَن لُباسُن
پَرِتِن حواسُم

جمع کن لباس‌هات
حواسم پرته

50

Come collect your cloths
I'm scatterbrain

سوزی مَزَن چو
بِهلی خُوَد اَرو

شترم را با ترکه نزن
بگذار خودش می‌رود

There is no need to strike my camel
Let it go on its own

نِشتی رو حوضی
چِمِ گُحتِہ غَیضی؟

52

روی لبه حوض نشسته‌ای
چه گفته‌ام
که قهر کرده‌ای؟

You sit by the edge of the pool
What did I say that
Made you upset?

لَشُم بَریه کوه
دَستی خُوَدُم سوح

جنازه‌ام را به کوهستان ببرید
دستی دستی خودم را سوختم.

Take my body to the mountains
I set myself ablaze
With my own hands

گُدَرَک بیدُن
ای‌سر ناومیدُم

54

گذرگاه درختان بید
ناامیدم، ناامید!

Along the path of the willow trees,
I go with no hope!

مالک شَوَدَشتِن
چورو به گشتِن

رمه به شبچر است
چوپان
به تنهایی

55
____

The flock is grazing at night
The shepherd being lonely

تا یاد اَکَحَم
مُ خُب نابَهَم

تا زمانی که به یاد تو می‌افتم
بهبود پیدا نخواهم کرد

So long as I dream of you
I cannot heal

56

مَرَه که شَوِن
جُنُم زیر تَوِن

نرو که شب است
و
تنم سراسر تب

57
____

Don't leave, it's nighttime
And a fever runs through my whole body

تَحتیهِ پای سایهَت
جُنُم کَن راحت

در سایه‌سار خانه‌ات
تختی است
جانم را بگیر و راحتم کن

58

In the shadow of your house
There is a bed
Take my life and set me free

ماشینی رَد بو
بهداری اَد بو

اتوموبیلی شتابزده گذشت
روبه‌روی بهداری
کوبید روی ترمز

A car drove past in a hurry
Stepped on the break
Before the village hospital

هوا بهارِن
چِشمُم گَهارن

هوا بهاری است
چشمم
نگهبان جاده

60

Spring is in the air
My eye is watching the road

اِمرو دوروزِن
نَهشُم داگ روزِن

امروز روز دوم است
که جنازهام افتاده
بر تفت آفتاب

Today is the second day
That my corpse is
Lying under the sun

در خونه‌ی دوستُم
ناهِلِن وَیَستُم

دم در خانه معشوقم
نمی‌گذارند
که بایستم

62

I am before the house of my beloved
They do not let me stay for long

جنگ تو مُگُنِن
ای‌سر خُوَمُنِن

نزاعی در نخلستان
به خاطر
ماجرای من و تو

In the palm fields a fight breaks out
Over the story of you and me

زیر ساگ لیمبورُن
منزل مودبورُن

در سایه‌سار درختان بلند لیموست
خانه‌ی زیبایان

The house of fair maidens
Is in the shadow of tall lemon trees

چایی جفت کَندِن
ناشتا و رَگبندِن

یک جفت قند
کنار استکان چای
سر بساط چای

A pair of sugar cubes
By a cup of tea
On the tea mat

تو باگ تنباکی
مودبور میلاکی

زیبارویی
با موهای بور بافته
در باغ تنباکو

66

A fair-faced maiden
With golden locks
In tobacco fields

أَوریَه به سَر یَح
مودبور ای در یَح

ابری در آسمان عیان شد
زیباروی من
از گرد راه رسید

A cloud appeared in the sky
My fair-faced love
Appeared amid the dust of the road

چارکَدِت واکَن
اشکونُم پاکَن

روسریت را باز کن
و پاک کن
اشک‌هایم را

68

Take off your scarf
And wipe off my tears

بیمار سالُم
ناپُرسی حالُم

یک سال است که بیمارم
و تو
حالم را نمی‌پرسی

I have been ill for a year
And you did not check up on me

کطال کمرِت
خیر بو سفرِت

قطار پوشیده‌ای
سفرت به خیر باد

You wear a bullet belt
Safe travel!

کورِ چشونُم
راه دَ نِشنُم

چشم‌هایم نابیناست
دستم را بگیر
و در راه بینداز

My eyes cannot see
Take my hand and show me the way

ماهَک شروگِن
ئیگَپ دروگِن

ماه در حال پرتو افشانی است
نه !
این فاجعه را باور نمی‌کنم

In a night with such luminous moon
I cannot believe this calamity

بالشتی کَوِتِه
سَهُبُشکی خوِتِه

متکایی افتاده
وسیاه گیسویی
سر بر آن گذاشته، در خواب است

A pillow on the floor
And a dark-haired beauty, her head on it, is asleep

درکَه سر بارریز
یاد کَه ای هما روز

از تپه بالا برو
و همان اتفاق را به یاد آور

Climb the hill
And remember that day

یَه‌گُم — دوگُم بیا
بالای مُگُن بیا

نرم بیا، با گام‌های آرام
قرارمان
بالای نخلستان

Tread softly with slow-paced steps
Meet me at the top of the palm fields

دَم دَم بَیومیه
نَمبُ گُمُنیه

دمدمای سحر بود
همچین اتفاقی را
پیش‌بینی نمی‌کردم

76

Dawn was in the air
I was not expecting this

نکن کنارَه
نایام دوباره

از من کناره نگیر
برای بار دوم
برنمی‌گردم

77

Do not stay away from me
I won't come back a second time

دَمزِن و پُلکِن
روبَار مَی مُلکِن

سراسر گرد و غبار
سرزمین من است
رودبار

Sand and dust throughout
This is Roudbar, my land

چادِن کَشورُن
زنده به گورُم

گوشه‌ی چادرت
کش می‌خورد بر خاک
مرا زنده به گور می‌کنی

79

You drag your chador
through the ground
It buries me alive

خال کو جَگِرُم
ساگ کَن نَمِرُم

جگرم سیاه شد از تفت آفتاب
پیکرت را سایه‌ام کن
تا که زنده بمانم

The scorching sun is killing me
Only the shadow of your body
Can save me

اِستالک شوکَش
بودُم درازکَش

ستاره‌ی سحر که سر زد
جنازه‌ام فرش زمین شد

81

As the morning star arose
My corpse collapsed on the ground

کَطال کَمرِت
پَهنِ خبرِت

خبر مسلح شدن‌ات
همه جا پیچیده است

82

The tale of you bearing arms
Has spread everywhere

ساعتِ چارِن
سر روپای یارِن

ساعت، چهار
سرم بر زانوی یار

It's four in the morning
My head is on the knee of the beloved

سورِگگ داکین
تَهنای چه باکین

شوره‌زاری‌ست بی‌انتها
چه باک از تنهایی

It's an endless marsh of salt
Yet I dare to be alone

دسکو رو سَر یاو
دَل مَ خُورِه تاو

دختر به لب رود می‌رود
دلم افتاده به پیچ و تاب

The girl walks toward the river bank
The wind starts blowing in my heart

نَنِن دِل اَی دِل
خَلَکیت کِ بد دِل

اینقدر روبهرویم ننشین
مردم را به شک انداختی

Don't sit so long in front of me,
People have begun to wonder

86

یاو رو کون کَرتُن
نُمزادی بُرشُن

جوی آب
در زیر بوته‌ی کَرت‌ها پنهان شد
نامزدش را بردند

87
——————

The water canal
Flows hidden behind the bushes
They took his fiancé away

رو نِشِت، پَسین بو
شین‌زَرد نِگون بو

آفتاب غروب کرد
پیراهن زرد نقش زمین شد

As the sun set
The yellow dress fell on the ground

غوری کِر آتِش
ای مُنِت تَهنا هِشت

قوری چای گوشه‌ی آتش
تنهایم گذاشتی

Tea pot lies beside the bonfire
You have left me alone!

شَوَک تَهارماه
بُرشُن بَی شورگاه

90

در شبی‌که ماه تاریک بود
جنازه‌اش را به شورگاه بردند

On the night of a dark moon
His corpse was taken to the morgue

تو تَنگ گیشُن
پابَه کُل دیشُن

دره، درختان گیش
بلند شو، همه دیدندمان!

The valley, oleander tress!
Get up! We've been seen!

زندُن سیم خاردار
خُوَت کِه گرفتار

زندان، با سیم‌های خاردار
خودت را گرفتار کردی!

92

Prison and the barbed wire
What have you done to yourself?

شوَک چه ماهِن
وَعد گُل صباحِن

شب مهتابی زیبایی است
قرار من و گل فردا است

93

There is a beautiful full moon
My flower and I will meet tomorrow

بُشکی رو اَوری
نِهَم هِشتوری

موهایش افتاده روی ابروها
سخت بیمارم!

Her hair hangs over her eyebrows
I am gravely stricken!

مُردِن پَسینی
لاشهَم نبینی

دم غروب مُردم   95
خدا کند که جنازه‌ام را نبینی   ─────

I died upon the setting of the sun
May you not see my corpse!

جنگل کَهوری
تَهنای دِلکوری

جنگل کهور
تنهایی
با دل کور

96

Kahour forest
Alone
With a black heart

تفنگ به کَنگی
ووستادَر جنگی

تفنگی بر شانه داشت
ایستاده بود
و در پی شر می‌گشت!

Standing,
A rifle on his shoulder
Looking for trouble!

بُرمَک اِستالن
وادَی تو زالُن

چشمک زدن ستاره‌ها
قرار در نیزار

Under the twinkling stars,
A clandestine date in the bed of reeds

سورِگ دوریایی
سَحتِن جِدایی

در این شوره‌زار دور از آب
سخت است
فراق

99

In the salt-land far from water
So hard to be away from my love

نشستُم سر جَدَه
گذشت اَی وَدَه

100

سر جاده نشستم
از وعده‌ات گذشت

I sat on the road
The time you had promised to come
has passed

جنگل پیچچاکی
سبزه‌ی میلاکی

جنگلی انبوه
از پیچک‌های درهم
سبزه‌رویی با موهای بلند بافته‌شده

Dense forest
From the tangled ivy
There appears a tawny woman
With long braided hair

سر راهِت نشستُم
مث گوشت برشتُم

بر سر راه تو نشستم
و مثل گوشت برشته شدم

I waited for you on your pathway here
My skin charred under the sun

سُهتم، بِرشتُم
سر کولِت نِشتُم

سوختم و برشته شدم
اما
همچنان بر سر عهد تو مانده‌ام

My skin was charred
But I kept our promise

هرچی اگَردُم
حل نابو دردُم

با این همه سفر
باز
فراموش کردن این داغ
خارج است
از توان من

Wandering, as though it helps
To cart your love, from my chest

دست بیار خاطرُم
مو ای تو بار دلُم

خاطرم را آرام کن
قدری
از تو دلگیرم

Calm me down
You bewilder me

بسکی کِردُم سَیل
نیدادُم رو مَیل

از بس که خیره‌اش شدم
محلی به من نگذاشت

106

I stared at her over and beyond
She paid me attention, short of none

بُرشن لُباسُن
پرتِن حواسُم

رخت‌های عروس را بردند
هوش و حواسم را
از دست داده‌ام

They stole the bride's garments
I lost all sensibility

107

دروای زیرُن
بدجایه گیرُم

ورودی درختچه‌های زیر
به مخمصه افتاده‌ام

108

All around mesquite shrubs
I'm stuck

بسکی یَه و رو
راهیه مِیُن کو

اینقدر آمد و رفت
که کورهراهی در میانه پیدا شد

He came so many times and returned
That a pathway emerged in the desert

سُهریه دمیلِن
پاونُم به جیلِن

اتومبیلی سرخ‌رنگ در میان بیابان
پاهایم را به زنجیر کرده‌اند

A red automobile in the middle of the desert
They have chained my feet

تو اَی چپ، مُن ای راست
هر چی خدا خواست

تو از چپ بیا
من از راست
هرچه باداباد

You take the right passage
And I'll take the left
What will be, will be

در خونه پیش کَن
چراگ خاموش کَن

درِ خانه را ببند
فانوس را خاموش کن

Let the door keep itself shut
And the lantern turned off

اُتاک بادگیرِن
دوستُم درگیرِن

اتاقی با بادگیر
محبوب من درگیر

113

A room with a windcatcher
Yet my beloved is busy

شیشه‌ی پُر اَی بو
یَهتَم خُو نابو

شیشه‌ای پر از عطر خریده‌ام
هر کار می‌کنم
مجالی پیدا نمی‌شود که بیایم

I bought her a jar full of perfume
And still, there is no chance of visiting

ای تَ نِهُم رَد
یا تَ، یا اَلحَد

از وصل تو نمی‌گذرم
یا تو
یا لحد گور

I will not let go from connecting
Either with you
or the gravestone

چراغِ خاموش کَن
سَرُم تو کوش کَن

فانوس را خاموش کن
و
سرم را در بغل بگیر

116
——————

Turn off the lantern
Cuddle me

راه کَو پُشت باگُن
نیستِن چراگُن

راه
در پشت باغ‌ها گم شد
نور فانوس‌ها پیدا نیست

The road has disappeared behind the farms
No light is in sight

بخت اَی مُ برگَشت
یوار سرُم گشت

بخت از من برگشت
که بعدازظهر
گذارم به آن حدود افتاد

Luck abandoned me
The afternoon
I arrived in that neighborhood

خدا کَن چارَه
دوربی دُوارَه

خداوندا، چاره‌ای کن
که دوباره دور شود

O God, find me a solution
For him to go far, far away

نُمجی لَشتُن
زو بیا سَح گَشتُم

میان نخل‌ها پنهان شده‌ام
زود بیا
داغ آفتاب کبودم کرد

I am hiding between the palm trees
Hurry up, the sun is burning me

پیش وَر بیومِن
دوستی تَمُنِن

سپیده‌ی سحر است
و این رابطه تمام

Dawn rises
And we are done

آهُم تو دِلشُن
نُمزادُم بُرشُن

آهم به دل‌هایشان بیفتد
نامزدم را بردند

122

Let my sigh curse their hearts
They took my fiancé

نشستُم کَشِ جو
شاید گُوَمی بو

لب جوی آب نشستم
شاید مجالی پیدا شود

I'm sitting by the stream
May it be that something changes

خلوت پای چینه
گُل دارِن کینه

حرف‌های محرمانه
در پای دیوار کاهگلی
همه لبریز کینه‌اند

124

Grudge buds,
By the [short] clay-wall

مُنُم چه گفتِه
دِلت اَی مُ گفتِه؟

من چه گفته‌ام
که تو دلگیری؟

What did I say
That you are saddened?

نیستی برابر
ناکُنُم باور

تو نیستی
و من
باور نمی‌کنم

You are not
and I
cannot believe

ای کوه به گودَه
گیضیِن ئی سوزه

از کوه به سمت دامنه
سبزه‌رو قهر است

Between the mountains and the slopes
The tawny woman is angry

بالا به گود بیا
روت نابو، شو بیا

از بالا به سمت پایین حرکت کن
اگر شرمت می‌آید
شبانه بیا

Come from top to bottom
If you are embarrassed
Thread at night

مار خُورده جونُم
مُ خُود اَدُنَّم

مارگزیده‌ام
می‌دانم که با من چه خواهد شد

A snake is eating my soul
No need for others to tell me
the fate I know myself

گِفتَم دُراگیه
برُم تو ساگیه

دردی در دلم پیچیده
مرا به سایه‌ای ببر

There is a pain in my heart
Take me to the shade

130

سر سورِگ حِلِه
چَرخی تَگِله

اول شوره‌زار به زانو درآمد
چرخ عمرش غلتید
و فرو افتاد

At the beginning of the salt marshes
The wheel of his life rolled away
He fell to his knees

گفتُم مَرَه شو
گپ مُنِت نَشنو

گفتم که شب نرو
حرفم را نشنیده گرفتی

132

I told you not to leave at night
You ignored my words

نِشتُم پای کودُم
دَستُنم اَسوزُم

پای اجاق نشسته‌ام
دست‌هایم را داغ می‌کنم

Sitting by the stove,
Branding my hands [by the fire]

کاصِد به رَندُم
هَنو دِلبندُم

قاصدی به دنبالم فرستاده‌اند
اما
هنوز دلبسته‌ی توام

A messenger has been sent after me
But
I'm still attached to you

تو ساگِ بادُم
گیضِن نومزادُم

در سایه‌سار بادام
نامزدم قهر است

135

Under the shadow of the almond tree
My fiancé is upset with me

کاگَذ تو پاکت
ندارُم طاکَت

کاغذی در پاکت
بی‌طاقتم

A letter in an envelope
I cannot take this anymore

لنگِت سراکَش
نفس اکَنین بَش

لُنگت را بر سر کشیده‌ای
با هم
نفس‌هایمان را تقسیم می‌کنیم

You put your peshtemal on your head
We share one breath

لُنگت مَده باد
بوی مِسک و زباد

لُنگت را بر باد نده
هوا پر می شود از بوی مشک و زباد

Do not let wind pass through your peshtemal
The air will fill with the smell of musk

دِسکوی سُرپَمی
نور تو خَشَمی

دختر لب سرخابی!
تو
نور این دهکده‌ای

139

Her crimson-coloured lips
Are the jewels of the village

تَ اَرَی مَ اَمونُم
وُرگِ پُت جُنُم

می‌روی و می‌مانم
موهای تنم شعله‌ور شده‌اند

140

You will go and I will stay
The hair on my body is on fire

سُرُنِ داگِت
شوروم اَیادت

لب‌های داغ تو
شب و روز به یاد توام

141

Your fiery lips
Are all I think about day and night

Translators' Biography

Mahdi Ganjavi is a distinguished historian specializing in education, literature, print, and translation within the Middle East. A former Postdoctoral Fellow at Northwestern University School of Education and Social Policy (SESP), he currently teaches at the Faculty of Information, University of Toronto. His work focuses on the transnational history of literature, education, translation, print and publication, the cultural Cold War and the politics of archive and historiography in contemporary Middle East. His scholarly writings have appeared in the *Encyclopaedia Iranica*, *Iranian Studies*, and *Review of the Middle East Studies*. Ganjavi's translation of high modernist, eco-poetry and New York School English poetry to Persian is published in several literary magazines such as *Neveshta* and *Namomken*. He has also contributed a translation to *Shades of Truth: Iranian Short Fiction of the Fifth Generation in Translation* (Mannani, M & E. Dehnavi Eds., Mazda, 2019).

Amin Fatemi is a teacher, translator, and Irish literature scholar. He studied at Trinity College Dublin and is currently finishing his PhD on the early work of Samuel Beckett and phenomenology at the University of Reading. He is the general editor of *Longitūdinēs*, a multilingual magazine for creative writing, literary translation, and the arts. He has taught courses on Samuel Beckett's prose, English and Irish poetry, poetic meter, and James Joyce's *Ulysses*. His current research focuses on the Irish language and literature written in modern Irish.

Mansour Alimoradi is a Persian-language poet from Roudbar. Alimoradi undertook an ethnological effort to record and translate the oral tradition of Roudbar into Persian. This effort is part of his wider contributions to the study of Roudbar's poetry, folk culture, and costumes.

Asemana Books is devoted to publishing diasporic,
underrepresented, and progressive literature on the Middle East.

asemanabooks.ca

ASEMANA
BOOKS